PEOPLE

Hilda Doran
Wilma McDonald
Paul Mills
Avis Swarbrick
Jim Wilson
Robert Wilson

Northern College of Education, Aberdeen

NOW! A project devised by Northern College of Education, Aberdeen
in conjunction with Occidental North Sea Consortium which comprises:
Occidental Petroleum (Caledonia) Limited
Texaco Britain Limited
International Thomson Plc
Union Texas Petroleum Limited
Published by Ward Lock Educational

Contents

People at Work   *Jobs today and jobs in the past*   3

Working 100 Years Ago   *Life for our great-grandparents*   4

Through the Generations   *Family histories*   6

A Helicopter Pilot's Day   *A personal diary*   8

The Winchman's Gear   *Equipment to save lives*   10

I am a Winchman   *A story in pictures*   12

Rescue At Sea   *A true story*   14

Paul 'Red' Adair   *The value of training*   16

Life on an Oil Platform   *Cooking and cleaning*   18

The Cabin Stewardess   *Work on a platform*   19

Oiling the Wheels of Industry   *Communication, supply, maintenance*   20

Four careers in a Lifetime   *Adapting to opportunities*   22

Centre Spread   *Teamwork*   24

Who is Mary Smith?   *One person from differing viewpoints*   26

Describing People   *Four sets of characteristics*   28

Night and Day   *Working unsocial hours*   29

Work and Leisure   *How people spend time off*   30

Offshore Meals   *Eating on a platform*   32

Meals for Special Occasions   *From around the world*   34

James 'Paraffin' Young   *The inventor of the refinery*   36

Edwin Laurentine Drake   *The first oil strike*   38

Newspaper Reports   *The five W's*   40

Testing Times   *Checking products are safe*   42

Workmates: A Game to Play   *Build up a team*   44

Vocabulary   46

Index   47

Acknowledgements   48

People at Work

One day in the future you will be looking at advertisements to try to find a job. Wouldn't you be surprised if you saw one for a knight's pageboy or a cabin boy on a sailing ship? Nobody does these jobs any more. They have disappeared along with others from the past.

Here are muddled lists of jobs. Some are from the past (before your grandparents were born), some are from the present and some could be found in both. Read the lists first.

disc jockey	doctor	chimney sweep
miller	jet pilot	nuclear physicist
steam engine driver	**roustabout**	dairymaid
cabin boy	astronaut	artist
blacksmith	town crier	saddler
knight	lamplighter	computer programmer

- Sort the lists out into two circles like this, only much bigger –

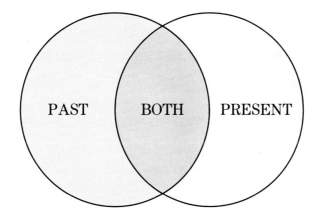

- Add any more jobs you can think of yourself that will fit the circles.

- Pick out two of the jobs from the past.

- Write down why you think these jobs died out.

- Make up an advertisement for one of the old jobs. Think carefully what kind of person you would want for a job like that.

Working 100 Years Ago

- Read about great-grandfather Sinclair on **Linemaster 12**.
- Underline the place names mentioned in his history and look them up in an atlas so that you are quite sure you know where they are.

His son, grandfather Sinclair, can remember when his father was getting ready to go away to sea again. This is what he says about those days –

'I always knew when it was time for him to go. His trunk was scrubbed out and put in the wind to dry. Mam had been knitting great thick socks for him, because all the ones he brought back were full of holes and smelled funny.'

- What do you think great-grandfather Sinclair would have taken with him on his journey apart from new socks?

Remember – he would be away 18 months
           – he was going to the Antarctic
           – there would be no shops

- Whaling is one of the jobs which has disappeared in Britain. Why do you think this is? For more information see *It's Your World* page 30.
- What do we use instead of whale oil nowadays?

 ● Read about great-grandmother Sinclair on **Linemaster 12**.

● How old was she when she got married?

● How did she earn extra money at home?

● Why do you think it was difficult for women like great-grandmother Sinclair to go away from their homes to work in those days?

Even today, Shetland is famous for its hand-knitted goods. Great-grandmother Sinclair knitted all her husband's jumpers and socks, as well as underwear! The jumpers were knitted in heavy undyed wool without too much of the natural grease, or **lanolin**, removed so that they would be waterproof. For 'best', however, jumpers were knitted with coloured patterns.

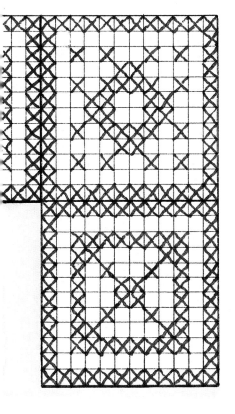

 ● Use squared paper to draw out one of the simple Shetland patterns like the one here with one colour on the graph paper. Then try some patterns with more colours.

● Repeat the pattern to fill up the whole page of squared paper.

● Try to invent a pattern of your own to use as a fancy border for a picture or a special card.

 ● Make a list of all the jobs the other great-grandparents of the other families did.

● Add to the list any jobs that the great-grandparents of any of your classmates have done or the jobs of your own great-grandparents, if you know.

Through the Generations

 ● Read about three British families on **Linemasters 12** and **13**.

 ● Complete a table like this with the names of all 24 people and the jobs they have done. Start with all the great-grandparents and end with all the great-grandchildren.

Name	First job	Second job
Great-grandfather Sinclair	Whaler	
Great-grandmother Sinclair	Hand-knitter	

● Look carefully at the table when it is finished.

● Underline all the jobs connected in some way with oil. How many are there?

● Who is the oldest person in your list connected with the **oil** industry?

● How old is this person? Which **generation** does the person belong to?

● Who is the youngest person on the list connected with the oil industry?

● How old is this person?

 ● Now read about the American family, the Willards, on **Linemaster 13**.

● With a partner, imagine a conversation between son Willard and son Green meeting for the first time on a plane.

Think of the kind of questions they might ask one another and the stories they might tell.

Write a script for the conversation.

Practise the accents.

● Tape record the conversation and play it back to the rest of the class.

1990
1980
1970
1960
1950
1940
1930
1920
1910
1900
1890
1880

- Choose *one* of the four families from the family histories.

- Draw out a Timeline like the one here which spans over a century. Put it down the middle of a page.

- At the left hand side of the Timeline put in the names of all the people in that family, with arrows pointing to where they were born.

At the right hand side of the Timeline mark, in the same way, the birth dates of people who are important in your life.

In many parts of the world, including Britain, a person's surname described the job he did.

Here are some examples: –

Smith	Butler
Cartwright	Sawyer
Potter	Carpenter
Weaver	Thatcher

- Do you know what all these jobs were? Look them up in a dictionary if you do not know.

Using your local telephone directory, scan the tops of the pages for other names linked to jobs. You will be surprised at how many you can find.

Because names are passed down from generation to generation it will be old-fashioned jobs you will find. The job may have gone, but the name remains.

Each area of the country has its own special jobs which might not be found anywhere else. Some might be dying out.

- Write a list of special jobs in your area.

- Pick one out of the list and write about it in as much detail as you can.

A Helicopter Pilot's Day

Helicopters are a very useful form of transport. Every day they carry people and **cargo**. They deliver urgently needed spares and fresh food to remote places. They are often used in emergencies.

Read this diary account of one helicopter pilot's working day flying to and from an oil platform in the North Sea.
Linemaster 14 gives the meanings of all the words shown in bold type. Keep it beside you as you work. (Some words have more than one meaning. The meaning given on the **Linemaster** is the one used in the diary.)

07.30 Reported for duty.
Co-pilot and I studied briefing sheet: destination, load, summary of weather conditions.
Calculated fuel needs for round trip.
Checked load – 16 passengers plus baggage outward, well within our maximum limit.

08.00 Pre-flight check of engines and all navigation equipment.
Passengers donned survival suits and boarded aircraft.

08.30 Take off. Visibility poor :– low cloud.
Guided out by Air Traffic Control.
Co-pilot navigated
 – radioed coastal stations and the platform for local weather report and details of return load.
 – wrote up flight log.
 – recorded readings on pressure and fuel gauges

10.45 Descended till we could see platform.
Positioned helicopter. Lowered undercarriage
Completed landing checks. Landed on helideck.

11.00 Passengers disembarked
Kept rotor blades turning to prevent twisting and other damage from sudden gusts of wind.

Refuelled.
Took on board passengers, cargo .... and breakfast for co-pilot and myself!

11.30 Handed over controls to co-pilot.
Take off: different return route to avoid outward traffic
Navigated. Did paperwork, including a Customs form (had been to International Waters.)

13.45 Over airport. Visibility poor.
Air Traffic Control positioned us for instrument landing.
Could just see runway from height of 70 metres — no need to divert.
Landed OK.
Total flight time : 5¼ hours

14.00 Final check of fuel and instruments before leaving aircraft. Aircraft to be refuelled, washed, cleaned and engine to be checked by ground crew.

14.30 Enjoyed a late lunch. Have completed my maximum of 100 flying hours this month, so am off flying duties the rest of this week.

- There are 10 sections in this story. Here are 10 titles, one for each section. Put the titles into the correct order.

Landing on the platform;   The return journey;   Helicopters' North Sea Work;   Landing at the Heliport;   **Pre-flight** check;   **Post-flight** check;   On the platform;   The outward journey;   Pre-flight preparation;   Take off from heliport.

- Use **Linemaster 15** to prepare some notes.

- Prepare a diary of a day in your own life.

- Make a collage of a helicopter pilot's view of an oil platform, using card shapes to form a silhouette of the platform as seen from the air, with the sea as background. Detail can be highlighted in crayon, paint, felt tip pen.

The Winchman's Gear

When a helicopter crew sets out on a rescue operation, they are never sure what will happen.

- Look at the picture opposite of a **winchman** in his **gear**. Use **Linemaster 14** to look up words you do not know.

- Which parts of the winchman's gear:
(a) protect him from water and cold?
(b) might be needed during a rescue?
(c) would be used if he lost contact with the helicopter?

- Why does he not carry any equipment in his hands?

- List the gear and equipment used by people in two other jobs.

Problem Solving

For the next activities you will find an instruction guide on **Linemaster 16**.

- Make a small model of a winchman from plasticine.

- Build a simple switch using drawing pins, paper clip, block of wood. Diagram (a) on **Linemaster 16**.

- Make a model winch to lower and stop your winchman. Diagram (b). You will need: –

small electric motor (for example, a Lego motor)
battery (or Lego battery power pack)
simple switch, thread, connecting wire

- If you have two batteries you can build a reversing switch so that you can lower or pull up your winchman. Diagram (c).

- If you have a Lego Technic kit you could try to make your winchman descend or rise more slowly using **gears**. Can you design a geared system of lowering and raising your winchman?

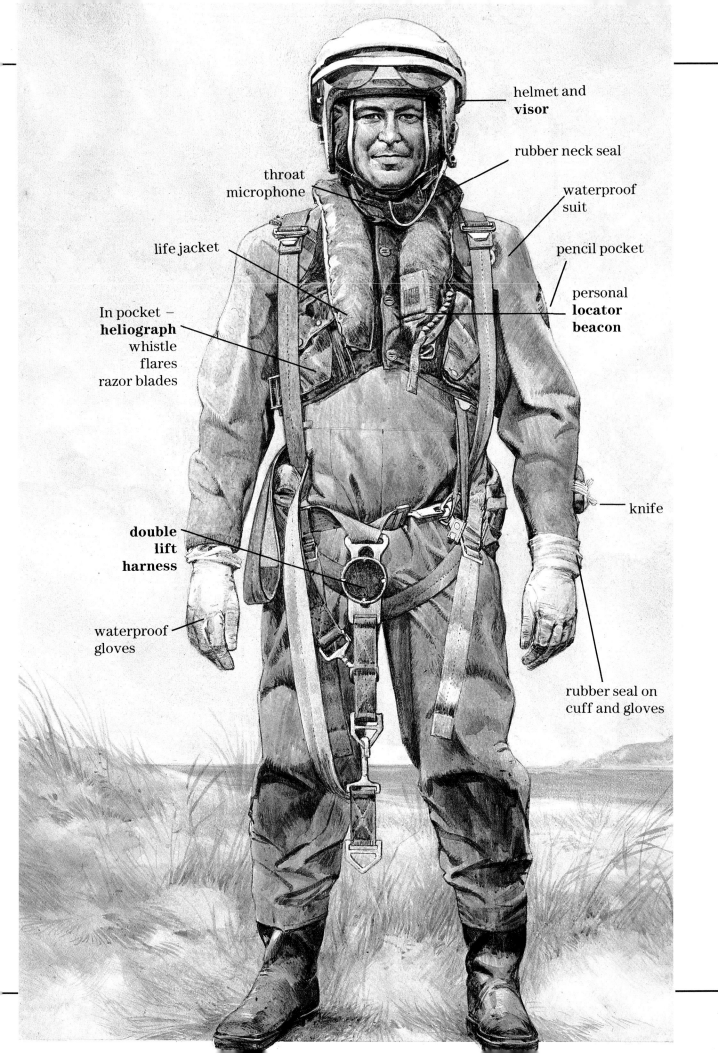

helmet and **visor**

rubber neck seal

waterproof suit

throat microphone

pencil pocket

life jacket

personal **locator beacon**

In pocket – **heliograph** whistle flares razor blades

knife

double lift harness

waterproof gloves

rubber seal on cuff and gloves

I am a Winchman

I'm often called a 'spider man'. Can you guess why. We carry out rescues on land and sea.

The command comes, 'Scramble'. The Pilot, co-pilot and the other winchman and I make for the helicopter.

My mate and I check the equipment for the rescue. We do a 'winch run out' to make sure it is in working order.

The pilots do a pre-flight check and then we are off.
We are all wearing survival suits.

We have to rescue an injured man on a supply ship. Before I go 'down on the wire' I strap on my double lift harness.

My mate is a skilled winchman. He directs the pilot over the tossing ship so that I can be lowered gently and safely.

While I am being lowered I risk being dashed against the side of the ship.

The harness is slipped over the injured man's shoulders. I support him with my legs as we sail upwards.

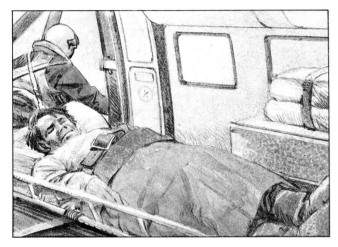

My mate and I help him into the helicopter. We stow the winch away, shut the door and head for the hospital.

Another rescue over! It is said that for every helicopter built seven lives have been saved.
I like my job.

 Use **Linemaster 14** to look up words you do not know.

● Imagine you are a reporter for your local newspaper. You have interviewed the winchman and the man who was rescued. Now write your report as vividly as possible. Look carefully at the pictures for interesting details which you could include in your story. (See pages 40–41 to help you to write a newspaper report.)

● Write a poem describing the ship in the storm. Here are some words to help you: –
trough, pitch, toss, roll, breaker, surge, swell, tremble, rattle, swing, roar, spray, foam, shudder, gale, howl, tempest.

Rescue At Sea

Working at sea can be very dangerous. Every year there are stories in the newspapers of accidents which happen to fishing boats and on oil **rigs**. Some of these stories have tragic endings. This one has a happy ending and is a true story.

One December evening, the crew of a Search and Rescue helicopter based at Sumburgh airport in Shetland got the call to go out to help a fishing boat in trouble off the Shetland coast. The boat was the *Elinor Viking*, an Aberdeen trawler.

● Read this extract from the helicopter captain's **Log** Book –

'Elinor Viking foundering on rocks in a **force 10 gale**. Very difficult to locate. Helped by a ship with searchlights. Boat found lying on its side. Crew on deck being pounded by waves. Lifted four on board, with boat breaking up. Lifeboat arrived but could not get close in. Uplifted remaining crew members.'

● Look at this photograph.

It is the *Elinor Viking* when it was launched.

● Read what the helicopter **winchman** said to reporters afterwards –

'The first time I went down on the hook, I got a bang on the head with the mast. That taught me to be a bit more careful. So we picked a better point on the **port** side and managed to get the crewmen up one at a time.'

● Now read what one of the crew of the lifeboat said –

'It was one of the most fantastic rescue operations there has ever been in this area. If it hadn't been for the helicopter I doubt if any of the fishermen would have been saved. The captain who went down on the hook did a marvellous job. But they were all heroes.'

Look at this photograph of the crew members after they were rescued.

 ● You now have all the information you need to write a newspaper article on the rescue of the crew of the *Elinor Viking*. (Pages 40–41 will help you to write your newspaper report.)

● Give you story a big banner headline.

● Write the story in narrow columns like a newspaper.

● Use your imagination to invent what the rescued fishermen might have said to a reporter after they were rescued.

● Draw pictures to go into your story.

 ● The wives and children of these rescued fishermen must have been very worried by the news of the *Elinor Viking* in trouble. Work in a group to plan a short drama about the homecoming of one of the fishermen.

Paul 'Red' Adair

1. In April 1977 disaster struck one of the oil platforms in the North Sea. There was a blow-out! Thousands of tonnes of oil spread out across the water. Gas filled the air. The first attempts to close down the well failed. A vital piece of equipment – the blow-out preventer – had been put in upside down. Immediately the company cabled one of the world's leading experts on oil well fires and blow-outs, Paul 'Red' Adair of Houston, Texas.

2. 'We'll fix it, just like any other blow-out. We've handled bigger and tougher wells than this.' 'Red' Adair spoke out confidently.

3. For two days a violent storm raged. When equipment could finally be landed on the platform, one method after another failed. At last the team managed to block the hole with metal tubing and to pump in a special heavy drilling mud. On the eighth day they flew home, their mission accomplished.

4. Since he started in business in 1959 he and his team have capped blow-outs and put out oil fires all over the world.

5. One of the most spectacular fires 'Red' Adair and his men extinguished was 'The Devil's Cigarette Lighter' in 1962 in the Sahara Desert. John Glen, one of the first astronauts said that he was able to see the blaze from his space capsule.

6. It is dangerous work. Explosives may have to be used to clear away damaged surface equipment to enable the team to make a close inspection of the scene. New wells may have to be drilled near the wild well to release the pressure. Often thousands of barrels of fluid have to be poured in to smother the blaze. The heat is intense, the flames burn the skin and there is always the danger of suffocation from the rain of falling ash.

7. 'Red' Adair developed his calm nerves and well planned approach to the task in hand when he was a bomb disposal expert in the second World War. Later he worked with Myson McKinlay the pioneer of oil well fire and blow out control.

8. 'Red' Adair makes sure that he and his team plan very carefully how they are going to do a job, and he insists that they obey the safety rules. Not one of his men has ever been seriously injured and they have never left a job uncompleted.

- Read the story about 'Red' Adair.
- Paragraph **6** describes how to cap a blow-out. List three things that the team might have to do.
- In paragraph **7** we are told that Red Adair
  (a) developed calm nerves
  (b) learned to plan carefully
  (c) worked with Myson McKinlay
Say how each of these would help him to do a good job.
- From paragraph **8** note down what Red Adair expects of his workers.

Red Adair believes that his staff must be properly trained.
Training can be hard work, it can be interesting, it can be repetitive and it can give you a sense of achievement because you begin to understand why things happen the way they do.

- Choose a team game and make a list of training activities. Divide them into two groups: those that are repetitive and those that help you to understand how things happen.
- Not all life is a game. In what skills are you being trained in school just now. Choose two that you would like to improve. Plan out carefully how you will do this – set yourself a target and tell the teacher when you have achieved it.
- In your school what rules would you make and how would you stop pupils breaking them?

- The story about Paul 'Red' Adair tells us little about him as a person and his way of life.
How could you find out more about him or anyone else who owns a company or is in the news?
- Build up a list of the places where this sort of information can be obtained.

Picture-making – a collage, a painting or wax crayons graffito of a blowout.
Use strong angry colours.

Life on an Oil Platform

Oil companies, like many other businesses, employ other firms to be responsible for cooking and cleaning on an oil **platform**. The person in charge of these jobs is called the "Camp Boss", is a qualified chef and probably has had experience in hotel management.

 ● Read this page and look at **Linemaster 17**.

Cooking staff

Head Chef – supervises food preparation and the work of the kitchen staff.

Baker – usually works during the night making rolls, bread, cakes and biscuits.

2 Cooks – qualified chefs trained to hotel standards.

Galley Stewards – wash pots and pans and help with the preparation of salads.

Mess Stewards – lay and clear tables.

Cleaning Staff

Chief Steward – supervises the cleaning staff.

Laundry Steward – operates the machines that launder personal and heavy duty clothing.

Cabin Stewards – clean all the living quarters.

The Cabin Stewardess

I am a cabin stewardess on an oil platform. I work a 12-hour day for a fortnight and then I have a fortnight at home.

Here is my daily timetable

07.00 – 09.00	Clean night-shift cabins – make beds, change towels, hoover, empty dustbins
09.00 – 09.30	Breakfast
09.30 – 12.30	Clean day-shift cabins, bathrooms and showers
12.30 – 13.00	Lunch
13.00 – 14.30	Clean stairs and corridors
14.30 – 15.00	Clean five offices
15.00 – 15.30	Tea break
15.30 – 17.30	Newspapers have arrived by helicopter. Deliver newspapers. Check laundry.
17.30 – 1800	Evening meal
18.00 – 19.00	Tidy the cabins of night-shift workers.

After work on fine evenings I can put on a hard hat and special shoes and go for a breath of fresh air on the helideck. In wet and stormy weather I spend my leisure time in the recreation room.

● Copy this grid about the life of the cabin stewardess and complete it.

	Eating	Cleaning and tidying	Other tasks	Leisure and sleeping
Number of Hours a day				
Total				

● Make a pie-chart which shows how the stewardess spends her day.

● The cabin stewardess has given a detailed account of her daily timetable. Write out the timetable for a day in your life and construct a grid showing how your time is spent.

Oiling the Wheels of Industry

Every business – needs to communicate with suppliers and customers
– needs materials to work with
– needs machinery and equipment kept in good working order.

Read how three people help to do this in the **offshore** oil industry.

Radio Operator

An offshore platform is a lonely island of activity. My job is to provide links with head office and with the ships and aircraft in the area.

On my platform I work alone on a 12-hour shift. The radio room operates 24 hours a day. I have three radios.

In the radio room we also have a **radar** unit which pinpoints the position of all ships in the area. We have a telephone and **telex** links too.

In an emergency I would be one of the last people to leave.

I suppose you could say I am the voice and ears of the platform.

Supply Boat Officer

My job is interesting whether I'm in port or at sea. My main task is to supply oil platforms with everything they need and to take away refuse, scrap metal, unwanted supplies and broken machinery.

Before leaving port, I have to make sure that the **cargo** is properly loaded and that our deck cargo of drill pipes and metal containers is chained down.

At the platform, the ship is unloaded without being tied to a berth, and I have to keep her steady. In bad weather we often have to wait near the platform for several days until the sea calms down.

Mechanical Specialist

My job is to keep all the equipment and machinery on the oil platform in working order. If there is a breakdown we have to work flat out until it is repaired even if this means going without sleep. However, we don't wait for a breakdown to happen – all our equipment is regularly checked and tested.

Before starting on any job I have to make certain that I know what to do and how the equipment works. The platform carries lots of spare parts. In an emergency they may be delivered by helicopter or we may even make them ourselves.

My colleagues and I work as a team and we take pride in keeping the platform in good working order.

● Now try **Linemaster 18**.

Here are three people in other jobs who communicate, supply and do **servicing**.

● Who are the people in your school who do these jobs?

Four Careers in a Lifetime

In times past, many people had the same job all their working lives. Now people often have to change jobs and learn new skills.

● Read this true story about one person who changed his job several times.

Ray Braithwaite's parents had a fish and chip shop in a small Yorkshire town.

He was interested in engines, and in his spare time he used to help out at the local garage.

When he left school he was an **apprentice** to a decorator and signwriter.

But he wanted to travel, so as soon as he was old enough he joined the navy as a boy apprentice.

He married while he was in the Navy.

For 13 years he travelled the world in the Navy. He enjoyed **servicing** machinery, and he was promoted.

He left the navy when his children were young, and for five years managed a caravan site. He moved caravans, fixed up their water and electricity supplies, built roads and drains, and mended machinery.

When the oil boom started, he saw an opportunity to get a job with better prospects. He signed on as a **roustabout**. He worked 12-hour shifts every day for a fortnight then he had a fortnight's break at home.

It was difficult being away from home so much. His family missed him and he missed them.

To widen his experience, he took a job in the **pump room**, helping to mix and control **drilling mud**.

He then became a **derrickman**, a dangerous and skilled job. He worked 50 metres up in the derrick, organising the supply of drill pipes to the drilling crew.

He studied in his spare time when he was at home. He was offered promotion to **assistant driller**, but was more interested in what was happening on the sea bed.

Now he is a **sub-sea** engineer. He directs the placing of drilling equipment on the sea bed. He is on call 24 hours a day. He holds the safety of the divers and the platform in his hands. It is a very demanding job.

His three children are now married, and he has three grandchildren. They live near him, so he sees them when he is **onshore**.

- What were Ray's four 'careers'?
- All through his life he kept up his interest in mechanics and engineering. How did this pay off in the end? What is the worst part of his present job?

- What is *your* main interest? What are you learning from it that might be useful to you when you are older?
Have you any ambitions? – write about them.

- These people work in teams. Link up with some of your friends, make up a team, and show how you work together.

- Observe each team in action. Choose one team and invite them to pose while the rest of the class sketches them. Square

- Square off one small area of your sketch and enlarge it so that it becomes a detailed close-up.

Who is Mary Smith?

Here are Mary Smith's two children, Peter and Pamela. They think she is kind and fair – most of the time. But sometimes she is very strict. She makes them do jobs around the house. She expects them to work hard at school.

Here are Mary Smith's parents. They remember her when she was a little girl. She was rather untidy and a bit of a tomboy. She was always good at maths. She was interested in sport and she read lots of books.

Here is Mary Smith.

She is a computer programmer.

These are Mary Smith's colleagues at work. They think Mary is good fun. She works hard, but looks forward to getting home to her family. Her colleagues envy the exciting holidays she arranges with her family.

These are Mary Smith's neighbours. They think she is a good housewife and mother, but rather a dull person. She is quite helpful if someone asks her, but she doesn't have much time for gossip or friendly chats over the fence.

This is Mary Smith's passport. She needs it when she goes abroad on holiday or on business.

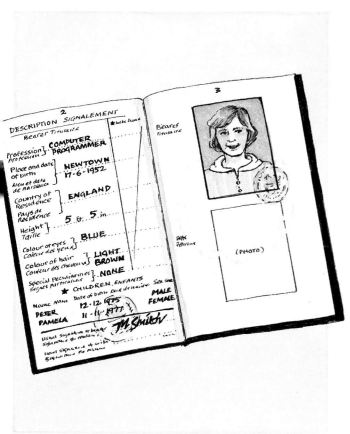

When Mary Smith applied for her present job she had to tell her employer about her education, her previous work experience and her interests.

All this information is given on what is called a CV – a 'curriculum vitae'. This is a Latin term meaning 'the story of your life'.

```
Name: Mary Smith
Address: 20 Bright Street, Newton,NT10 9TP
Telephone Number: (home) Newton 74536
Date of Birth: 17 June 1952


Education;
1957-1971 Newton Junior and High School
1971-1974 Eastern University, BSc Mathematics
1974-1980 Open University, BSc Computer Programming

Previous Employment;
1981-1986 Part-time computer programmer,
          Deep Diving Company
1986-date Computer programmer,
          Tiptop Oil Company

Hobbies and Interests
Holidays to Spain, Germany, Yugoslavia
Fluent Spainish
Member of local Stockcar Racing Club

References;
Previous employment          Character
Personal Manager             Dr John Mayim
Deep Diving Company          High Street
                             Newton
```

Who are you?

● Draw a portrait of yourself. Select four different people or groups of people who know you well, for example, your family, your school friends, your teacher, your neighbours. Draw pictures of them and write down what you think they think about you. Now ask one of your school friends to write down what he/she thinks about you. Compare this account with the one you wrote.

● Copy the headings on Mary Smith's passport, and fill in the details. You will find these in her CV above.

● Make a passport for yourself.

● Why do you think the employer is interested in:
a) Mary's education
b) Mary's previous employment
c) Mary's interests outside her work?

If you were an employer, what would you look for when you were interviewing an employee?

Describing People

1. You can describe their

features

hair, eyes, nose, mouth
complexion, shape of
face

lank	sparkling		smooth
piercing	straight	tight-lipped	
curly rosy	aquiline		snub
sallow	long		round

2. You can describe their

build

	stocky		
tall	slim		stooping
	slender	fat	obese

3. You can describe their

clothes

casual	neat	clean
	tidy	fashionable
	colourful	

4. You can describe their

character

when you get to know
them

strong	happy	
	generous	cheerful
gloomy	weak	bad tempered

● Start collecting words which describe people under each of the four headings.
You will find them in the stories you read. Write them in your notebook.

● Choose four people in your school. Look at them very carefully. On a piece of
paper write a short description of each without giving the name.

● Select from your reading what you think is the best description of a person.
Write this description on a piece of paper for a class booklet 'Describing People'.

Night and Day

Not everyone is up during the day and goes to bed at night. Some jobs have to be done 24 hours a day. Other jobs are done in the evening and at night when the rest of us are either relaxing or are asleep. The stories below are about people whose jobs mean that they have to work evenings, or nights, or weekends.

It is late evening when these railway workers begin their night's work, checking and repairing railway tracks. Many people work through the night so that others are able to work the following day.

Early evening, and the night's work is just beginning for fairground workers. Many people work at night and at weekends so that other people who have worked more normal hours during the day can go out and enjoy themselves.

Midnight on December 24, and some people are at work, making sure that electricity is available throughout the country. Many workers do jobs which ensure that essential services are available night and day.

- Make a list of all the jobs you know of that are done in the evening or at night.

- Sort out your list into:
(a) jobs done at night which help other people do their job the following day
(b) evening and night-time jobs which enable other people to enjoy themselves
(c) jobs which keep essential services running night and day.

- Suppose that you had to do one of the jobs which you have listed. Which would you decide to do, and why?

Work and Leisure

Some people work so many hours each week that they have little or no time for leisure. Other people, retired or unemployed, may find that they have too many hours to fill. People spend their leisure hours in very different ways. The stories below will give you some clues about what makes people spend their leisure time the way that they do.

Me and My Hobby

'My Dad had a milk round when I was young and I grew up with horses. I like them a lot, and in my present job I can afford to own one. I take him to horse shows. He's my most reliable friend.'

'I've always liked anything mechanical. I fix boat engines all day and do up old cars for a hobby at night.
It's a hobby that pays well too – I earn enough from it to pay for my annual holiday.'

'There's no work for me around here, so my hobbies have to be cheap ones. I like seaside walks with a few friends. It was my gran who got me interested in cliffs and beaches.'

'Engine driving is a strain. I need to relax afterwards, so I find a quiet place and do some fishing.'

'I have a dull job in this office block. I love growing beautiful flowers. It is interesting and satisfying. I often win prizes and get my photo in the paper.'

'I love company. Farming can be a lonely job so when I get the chance I like to go with my friends to a football match.'

People's leisure activities can give them the chance: –
to keep fit   to feel important   to earn money
to have company   to use their skills
to be with animals   to travel   to win things   to relax
to get away from their normal surroundings
to impress other people   to meet important people
to help less fortunate people

- Which of these reasons are given by the people whose stories you have read?

- Draw a picture of yourself at work, and at leisure.

- Write about your reasons for enjoying your own leisure activities.

- Draw a picture of yourself at work and at leisure in 10 years time.

- Be prepared to explain why you think that you will be spending your work and leisure time in the way that you have drawn.

Offshore Meals

When people working on a rig offshore are tired after their long working day, they cannot go home to their families. To make up for this, the cook and his staff offer tempting and attractive food at all times of the day and night.

Usually people either queue up for hot food, or choose cold food from the buffet. But on special occasions, such as Christmas, they do not queue up. The **galley stewards** serve a festive meal to them, one course at a time.

Here is the Christmas Menu from an oil production platform.

Christmas Menu

From The Galley

Hors D'oeuvre
Melon Balls in Wine
Terrine of Game
Seafood Cocktail

Soup
Scotch Broth
Cream of Tomato

Fish
Baked Haddock Meunière
Fillet of Sole

Main Course
Roast Turkey with Nut Stuffing
Minute Steak Garni
Smoked Virginia Ham

Vegetables
Roast Potatoes : Duchesse Potatoes
Brussel Sprouts : French Beans

Dessert
Sherry Trifle : Peach Gateau
Blackcurrant Cheesecake

Cheese
Selection of Cheeses

Coffee
Coffee   Chocolate Mints

From the Buffet
Dressed Tay Salmon
Crown of Lamb
Scotch Rib of Beef
Whole Boned Chicken
Prawns on Cracked Ice
Suckling Pig
Honey Glazed Duckling

Salads

Russian Egg : Waldorf
American : Coleslaw
Green Salad : Cucumber
Onion : Egg Mayonnaise
Potato : Beetroot

From the Sweet Trolley
Black Forest Gateau
Lemon Mousse
Strawberry Shortcake
Scotch Trifle
Crème Caramel

Fresh Fruit Basket
After Eight Mints
Dates

The buffet is a selection of cold dishes. All the workers help themselves to whatever they want.

The sweet trolley offers a selection of desserts for self service.

The buffet on the Christmas menu offers 10 different salads.

- Find the recipes for four of these salads. Write out the recipe for the one you like best.
Either draw and cut out a big plate in card, and on it make a tempting salad collage
Or bring in the ingredients and make a real salad.

Each country has its traditional desserts, created to make the best use of foods that are easily available.

- Find the names of the countries from which the recipes for these desserts come:

Black Forest Gateau	Pumpkin Pie
Scotch Trifle	Baklava
Simnel Cake	Savarin
Pavlova	

- Draw, colour and cut out your favourite sweet.

- Use your cut outs to make a large collage of a sweet trolley on your classroom wall.

The Galley Meal

- How many courses are in the Christmas meal? (Remember that the vegetables are served with the main course.)

- Many terms used in cooking are French. Find the meaning of these in a cookery book:
(a) Hors d'Oeuvre (b) meunière (c) garni (d) terrine (e) gateau

- In order to keep strong and fit everyone should eat some food that contains *protein*. Protcin is found in *Meat*, *Poultry*, *Fish*, *Eggs*, *Milk*, and *Beans*. List the protein dishes in the Christmas Menu under these headings.

Meals for Special Occasions

- As you read, make a list of the different foods the Pilgrim Fathers and the Indians brought to the feast.

Work on oil platforms goes on night and day, week in and week out, throughout the year. For the workers the pattern of life is unchanging. Every day is like every other day. National holidays and anniversaries could go unnoticed except for the changing menus. The chef cooks special dishes to celebrate special events and as workers come from all over the world, he has plenty of opportunities to use his skills and imagination. Americans would certainly expect a traditional Thanksgiving Dinner. Here is an account of how this celebration came about.

Thanksgiving Day Dinner

In 1620 the Pilgrim Fathers arrived in the sailing ship *Mayflower* from England and settled in what is now called Massachusetts. The winter that followed was bitterly cold. The 100 settlers were often hungry. More than half of them died. In spite of this they planted their crops. In 1621 there was a plentiful harvest. Moreover the Pilgrims had made friends with the Indians. They could now live in their new land in peace and plenty. To celebrate their good fortune the Pilgrims decided they must set aside a day to thank God for the plentiful harvest. For the feast the men shot wild turkeys and ducks. The Indians brought along deer they had hunted in the forest. From the sea the men took clams, oysters and lobsters; from the fields the settlers harvested peas, greens, corn and pumpkins; from the neighbouring bogs they gathered cranberries. That first 'Thanksgiving Feast' lasted three days.

- Now make up a traditional Thanksgiving Day menu. It should include dishes containing the foods on your list. Illustrate your menu attractively.

Nowadays Thanksgiving Day is always on the fourth Thursday of November. It is a national holiday when American families and friends can gather to give thanks for the blessings of the past year and to enjoy a meal similar to the one prepared by the first Pilgrims.

Other Special Occasions

● Workplaces and big hotels in all parts of the world cater for different religious groups. Find out the special dishes that are prepared for these festivals:

Festival	Religion	Food
Passover	Jewish	
Diwali	Hindu	
Easter	Christian	

Try to add to this list.
Make up a 'Round the World' menu. Every dish must come from a different country or be associated with a particular religious group.

● One of the most colourful festivals is the Chinese New Year.
Chinese cookery is said to be among the best in the world.
At every meal, they serve many dishes.
Try to get a copy of a menu from a local Chinese restaurant or ask the proprietor to come to talk to your class.
Collect the names of Chinese dishes.
Find their recipes.
Make a note of unfamiliar ingredients and try to find out about them.
Find out how the Chinese prepare and cook their food.
Prepare a Chinese meal and eat it in the traditional Chinese way.

James 'Paraffin' Young

The first oilman

● To learn about the life and work of James Young, the first oilman, read the numbered boxes in order.

6 Oil from Shale

1864 – **West Calder** Scotland – new factory to produce oil from **shale** – business expands

1870 – retired – continued to investigate and experiment to find the speed of light

1883 – died

5 Oil from Coal

1850 – **Bathgate** Scotland – patented his method of producing paraffin, lubricating oil, candle wax from coal

1858 – world's largest manufacturer of coal oil – nicknamed 'Paraffin' Young by Livingstone

1861 – visited America to collect royalties from firms using his process – went to Titusville to see first oil well

stocks of suitable coal being used up

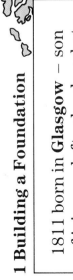

Bathgate

1 Building a Foundation

1811 born in **Glasgow** – son

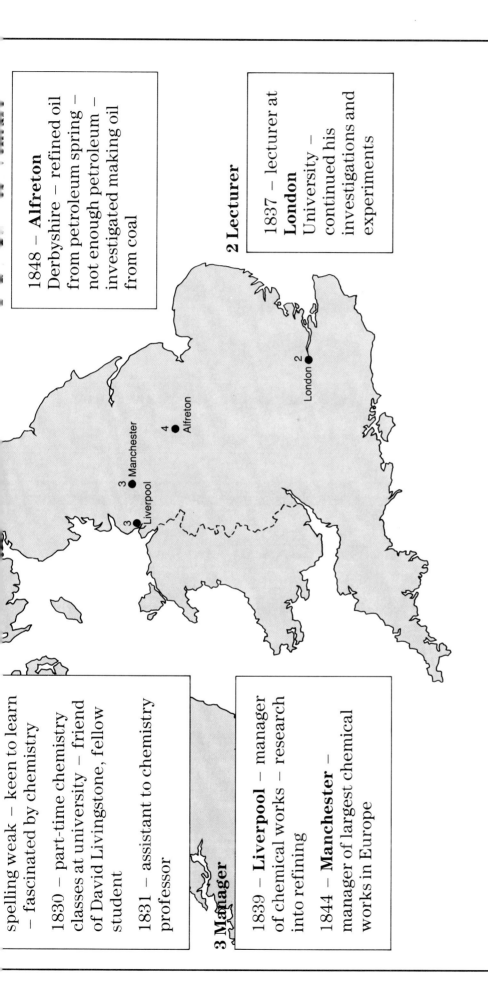

1848 – **Alfreton**
Derbyshire – refined oil from petroleum spring – not enough petroleum – investigated making oil from coal

2 Lecturer

1837 – lecturer at **London** University – continued his investigations and experiments

spelling weak – keen to learn – fascinated by chemistry

1830 – part-time chemistry classes at university – friend of David Livingstone, fellow student

1831 – assistant to chemistry professor

3 Manager

1839 – **Liverpool** – manager of chemical works – research into refining

1844 – **Manchester** – manager of largest chemical works in Europe

Manchester

Liverpool

Alfreton

London

- Write a biography of James 'Paraffin' Young. Write six short paragraphs using the title of each box as your main idea.

- Present James Young's life in music or movement and music. The music should reflect the places where he worked and his investigations and discoveries.

- Enlarge the map given on **Linemaster 19** and put it up on the classroom wall. On it mark some of the places you have learned about in this project.

19

Edwin Laurentine Drake

 ●Often in your studies you will want to find out about famous people and what they have done. This will be made easier if you know how to organise your notes. Here is one way of doing it.

Read the following biography of Edwin Drake and make notes under the following headings: –

1 Why he is important.
2 How he became involved in this work:
   (a) When he first heard or thought about it.
   (b) What he did.
   (c) Results.
3 The kind of person he was:
   adventurous, imaginative, determined, unfortunate, happy, enterprising, foolish, clever. Think of other words.
4 Any other details which you think are interesting.

You can use these headings when you are researching other famous lives.

The First Man to Strike Oil

'They've struck oil! They've struck oil!' was the cry heard one Sunday afternoon in 1859 in Titusville, Pennsylvania, USA. Edwin Drake had drilled the first productive oil well in the western world.

Edwin Drake was born in 1819 in Greenville, Green County, New York, the son of a poor farmer. When he was 19 he decided 'to go West' working at whatever came his way. In Detroit he was a canal boat worker, hotel clerk and store clerk. Finally he was a conductor on the New York to New Haven railroad. In 1857 he lost this job when he became ill.

His career then took an unexpected turn. He was staying at a hotel in New Haven when he met James Townsend who was a **shareholder** in the newly formed Seneca Oil Company. This company had leased land in Titusville, Pennsylvania, where there were natural oil springs. For years this oil had been put into bottles and sold as a medicine. But now

scientists were beginning to experiment with it. James 'Paraffin' Young had shown that it could be used to make oil for lighting and for lubricating machines. Large quantities would be needed. Townsend persuaded Drake to buy shares in the Seneca Oil Company and to go to Titusville to see if he could find the source of the oil springs.

Drake had no idea how he was going to do this. He visited salt wells at Pittsburgh and Syracuse to learn about drilling methods. He and his family arrived at Titusville in 1858. At first he tried to *dig* a well near the main oil spring but this was unsuccessful. The following spring he employed William A Smith ('Uncle Billy') a skilled salt mine driller and his 15 year old son for $2.50 a day. They failed because the underground rock was so soft and sodden with water that the sides kept collapsing. The local people ridiculed Drake's effort and referred to the operation as 'Drake's Folly'.

Then Drake came up with the simple yet clever solution that enabled him to succeed. He suggested they drive several sections of cast iron pipe down to bedrock to act as a **casing** for the drill – a technique which is still used today. The drilling continued down to a depth of 20 metres.

One Saturday Smith and his son stopped work as usual. On the Sunday Smith returned to the well and to his amazement he saw a dark **fluid** floating on top of the water below the derrick floor. They had struck oil! They had proved that underground **reserves** of oil existed and that these could be obtained by drilling. The great **petroleum** industry had been born.

Drake stayed on in Titusville till 1863. Unfortunately the tide of his fortunes turned again. He lost all his money in buying and selling shares in oil wells and died a poor man in 1880 at Bethlehem, Pennsylvania. Later it was realised how much he had contributed to the birth of the oil industry and his body was taken back to Titusville where a splendid monument now honours his memory.

● Use your notes to write a short account of Drake's life.
● Write to the Drake Museum, Titusville, Pennsylvania, USA for more information about Edwin Drake and the first oil strike.

Newspaper Reports

The following newspaper report is based on the story on pages 38–9.

Titusville 28 August 1859

Yesterday dozens of people watched oil being drawn from a 20-metre well in Titusville Pennsylvania. Edwin Drake, director of drilling operations, said 'I smelt oil. I just got stuck in there and kept going.'

Working for the Seneca Oil Company, Drake **spudded in** on the banks of Oil Creek earlier in the year. A few metres down, the sides of the well collapsed and soft rock filled the hole. Drake refused to give in. Iron pipes were ordered and rammed down the hole.

'I call it **casing**,' said Drake. 'I ain't going to be beat by no doggone sand and water.'

Strike

On Sunday Drake's assistant, 'Uncle Billy' Smith, checked the well as usual. He saw oil floating a metre or so below the surface of the well.

'I ran to town hollering and shouting,' said Smith.

A crowd quickly gathered. Today more visitors are arriving by the hour.

Further drilling operations are planned. If more oil is found the company will start commercial production. New **refining** techniques imported from England will be used to produce lubricating oil, lamp oil and candle wax as well as tar and other products.

Doubts

Some experts warn that this find is a flash in the pan. The well will quickly dry up, and there is little hope of extensive oil **strikes**.

'That's all hogwash', pronounced Drake. 'This here oil will change the world.'

 ● Discuss how this newspaper report differs from the story on pages 38–39.
Who is it written for?
Why is it shorter?
What extra information is given?
How does the reporter include human interest?
How does the reporter show that there are two sides to the story?

The Five Ws

In a news article the most important information is given at the *beginning*. The first paragraph should answer the questions: –

WHO is involved?　　WHEN did it happen?
WHAT happened?　　WHY did it happen?
WHERE did it happen?

 ● Check whether this is true of the article about Drake.

Headlines

Collect some newspaper articles. Look at the headlines.
What is their purpose?
What kinds of words are left out?

 ● Write a good headline for the story on the opposite page.

● Write a good headline for the story on pages 14–15 of this book, or for 'On the Rocks' which is on pages 18–20 of *It's Your World*.

Sub-headings

There are two **sub-headings** in the article opposite. They break the story into sections and tell you the main idea of each section.

 ● Look at the report opposite. Say where you might add two more sub-headings. Make them up. Use no more than two words for each.

Testing Times

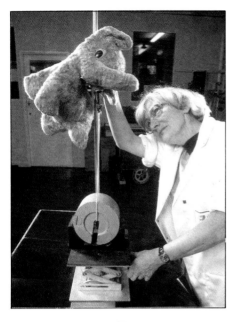

Congratulations! You got to school today! You have survived being a **consumer**. Your breakfast didn't poison you, the lights in the house didn't blow up when you switched them on and off, and your seat didn't collapse under you when you sat on it.

All of us make use of lots of things every day of our lives, and we take it for granted that none of the things we use will do us any harm – the wheels won't fall off the bus, car or train, our clothes won't catch fire in the sunlight, and hair shampoo won't make our hair turn bright green (unless we want it to!)

Firms carry out a programme of tests on their new **products**. In many cases, there are laws and regulations which state what a product must be able to do (and not do) before it can be sold. The product must be safe for people to use.

Safety regulations are very strict for two of the most well known products which depend on the oil industry – the motor car and the aeroplane.

When an airline places an order for a new fleet of aircraft, the buyer tells the manufacturer what he wants the plane to be able to do, for example, to be able to carry a certain number of passengers at a certain speed for a certain distance without having to refuel. This is known as the plane's *performance*.

No passenger aircraft is allowed to carry passengers until the aircraft has been put through all sort of tests which check that it can be flown safely. For these special tests, aircraft are flown by specially trained **test pilots**.

Jacqueline Auriol was a test pilot in France at the time when jet aircraft were first introduced in the years after 1945. She was 30 when she took her first flying lessons. Two years later she was so badly injured in a plane crash that doctors discouraged her two children from seeing her for almost two years whilst surgeons rebuilt her face. Brave Jacqueline

● Try and think of at least three tests that would be carried out on these six things before they would be considered 'fit for sale' and put into shops.

made up her mind to conquer the machines that had nearly killed her. She learned aerobatics, gained a licence to fly helicopters, and qualified as a gliding instructor. Within six years, after lots of hard work and studying, she became the first woman ever to be an official test pilot. By the time she retired, she had flown at more than twice the speed of sound and had held the women's world speed record on more than four occasions. She flew more than 180 different types of aircraft. A pioneer indeed!

 ● Pick out from this list the three words which you think best describe Jacqueline Auriol, and give a reason for each choice. Compare your choice with the choice made by others in the class.

adventurous   persistent   foolhardy
courageous   patient   determined   imaginative
adaptable   intelligent   belligerent

Aircraft are like any other **product** when it comes to trying to sell them to someone. Three main things about a product help to persuade people to buy it. These three things are: –

Performance – Will it do what I want it to do?
Price   – Is it good value, and can I afford it?
Punctuality – Will it be available when I want it?

 ● Make a paper aeroplane. (It is really a glider)
Before you begin –
Decide on what you want it to be able to do, for example, glide for a minimum of 5 metres when launched by hand from a height of 1 metre (vary this as much as you wish).
Give yourself a maximum target time in which to make it.
Design it in such a way that it uses up as little paper as possible.

 Fly your paper aeroplane along with those made by others.
The best paper aeroplane is the one which passes the performance test *and* has been made within the time limit *and* has used the least amount of paper (it is the cheapest to make).

Workmates: A Game to Play

To play this game you will need to make 10 sets of cards. Each set is about a different industry or service. Four jobs in each workplace have been chosen so you will make 40 cards.

The industries and services are: –

1. *Air Travel* – Pilot, Stewardess, Air Traffic Controller, Maintenance Engineer.
2. *Hospital Sevice* – Surgeon, Nurse, Porter, Radiographer.
3. *Postal Service* – Postwoman, Sorter, Counter Assistant, Driver.
4. *Newspaper Office* – Editor, Word Processor Operator, Reporter, Photographer.
5. *Supermarket* – Checkout Assistant, Shelf Filler, Butcher, Cleaner.
6. *Garage* – Mechanic, Petrol Pump Attendant, Paint Sprayer, Costing Clerk.
7. *Oil Platform* – Roustabout, Diver, Geologist, Cook.
8. *Police Station* – Policeman, Finger-print Expert, Dog Handler, Detective.
9. *Docks* – Fork Lift Driver, Docker, Crane Driver, Ship's Captain.
10. *House Building* – Plumber, Electrician, Bricklayer, Slater.

Number of players: 3 or more.

The aim of the game: to collect most sets of workmates.

To play the game, shuffle and deal all the cards face down. Players study their cards. The person to the right of the dealer, Player 1, begins by asking any other player for a particular card, naming the job and the industry or service. Player 1 must hold at least one of the workmates in the industry or service he is asking for. If the other player does *not* have the card he says so and he then can ask any other player for a workmate. If he does have the card he must give it to Player 1 and Player 1 can then ask any player for any

At the Airport

pilot, stewardess,
air traffic controller,
maintenance engineer.

other card to make up a set in his pack. He continues
to do this till he receives a 'No'.

Play goes on until all the sets are complete.

When a player has no more cards he is out of the
game. If he finishes by making a set, the player from
whom he took the last card continues to play. When
all the sets of workmates are complete the player
with the greatest number of sets is the winner.

At the Hospital

surgeon, nurse,
radiographer, porter.

At the Post Office

postwoman, sorter,
counter assistant,
driver.

At the Supermarket

checkout assistant,
shelf filler, butcher,
cleaner.

At the Police Station

policeman, dog handler,
finger-print expert,
detective.

At the Docks

docker, fork lift driver,
crane driver,
ship's captain.

At the House Builders

plumber, electrician,
bricklayer, slater.

At the Garage

mechanic, costing clerk,
petrol pump attendant,
paint sprayer.

On the Oil Platform

roustabout, diver,
geologist, cook.

At the Newspaper Office

reporter, photographer,
editor, word processor
operator.

Vocabulary

apprentice someone who is learning a job

assistant driller fourth in charge of drilling operations

blow-out dangerous uncontrolled eruption of gas or oil from a well

blow-out preventor valve that helps to prevent a blowout

capping closing a well to prevent the escape of gas or oil

cargo goods carried by ship, aircraft or lorry

casing pipes that stop the sides of a well caving in

consumer someone who buys something and uses it

dialect way of speaking in a particular district

derrickman member of the drilling crew who works high up in the derrick and controls the supply of drill pipes

drilling mud special mixture of clays, water and chemicals pumped down the well during drilling

drilling rig apparatus used to drill wells

drilling superintendent person in charge of the drilling operation

fluid anything that flows

force 10 gale most severe gale on the Beaufort scale of wind speeds

galley stewards people who help to cook and serve food on ships and platforms

generation all the people born at roughly the same time

industry business that produces something for sale

lanolin grease from a sheep's fleece

log record of events

offshore out at sea

onshore on land

petroleum mineral oil and what is made from it. The word means *oil from rocks*

platform large permanent structure used to control the recovery of oil or gas

port left side of a ship as you face forwards

product something made ready for use or sale

pump room room containing the mud tanks and mud pumps

radar television picture that shows where things are even in darkness, fog and mist

refining making crude oil ready for use

reserves quantity of oil which can be extracted from a well

round trip outward and return journey

roustabout manual labourer on a drilling rig

servicing checking equipment to make sure it is working properly and replacing worn parts

shale fine-grained rock laid down in layers which can contain oil

shareholder person who owns a part of a company and gets a share of the profits or losses

spud (in) start drilling

strike oil discover an oilfield

sub-sea underneath the sea

supply ship ship which takes supplies out to rigs and platforms

telex messages sent by telephone which are printed at the receiving end

test pilot someone who flies new aircraft to make sure that they are safe

winchman person who operates winches or is lowered by them

wild well well that has a blow-out

Index

Adair, Paul 'Red'   16, 17
aircraft   43
Alfreton   37
Antarctic   4
Auriol, Jacqueline   43

Bathgate   37
biography   39
buffet meals   32, 33

cabin stewardess   18, 19
celebration meals   32, 33, 34
Chinese cooking   35
communications   20, 21
cooking   32, 33, 34, 35
curriculum vitae   27

derrickman   23
describing people   26, 27, 28
Drake, James Laurentine   38, 39, 40
drilling   23
drilling mud   23

Elinor Viking   14, 15
engineer   23

family histories   4, 5, 6, 7
fishing   4, 14, 30

Glasgow   36

helicopter   8, 9, 10, 11, 12, 13, 14, 15
helicopter pilot   8, 9
hobbies   30, 31

jobs   3, 4, 5, 6, 7, 18, 19, 20, 21, 22, 23,
   24, 29, 30, 31, 43, 44, 45

knitting   5

leisure   30, 31
life stories   4, 5, 6, 7, 22, 23, 26, 27, 36,
   37, 38, 39, 43

Liverpool   36
London   37

Manchester   36
mechanical specialist   21, 23, 30
menu   32, 33, 34, 35

newspaper reports   13, 15, 40, 41

oil   4, 23, 24, 36, 37, 38, 39, 40
oil shale   36, 37
oil well   38, 39, 40

quality control   42, 43

radio operator   20
refining   35, 36
rescues   13, 14, 15, 16
roughneck   23
roustabout   23

safety   16, 17
services   21
Shetland   5, 15, 16
supplies   20, 21
supply ship 12, 20
surnames   7

testing   42, 43
Thanksgiving Day   34
timeline   7
timetable   18, 19
Titusville   38, 39, 40
training   16, 17

USA   6, 34, 37, 38, 39

whales   4
winchman   10, 11, 12, 13, 14, 15
work   3, 4, 5, 6, 7, 18, 19, 20, 21, 24, 25, 29, 30,
   31, 43, 45

Young, James 'Paraffin'   36, 37

First published 1988 by
Ward Lock Educational
47 Marylebone Lane
London W1M 6AX

A member of the Ling Kee Group
LONDON · HONG KONG · NEW YORK
SINGAPORE · TAIPEI

British Library Cataloguing in Publication Data

People: pupil text for the Now! project.
  1. Human ecology
  I. Doran, H.
  333.7   GF43

  ISBN 0–7062–4823–6

Designed by Eric Drewery, Bob Vickers and Adrian Singer
Typeset by GRP Typesetters, Leicester
Printed in Spain by Printeksa, Bilbao

Diagrams Ray Burrows
Illustrators Gay Galsworthy Centre spread
              Jenny Mumford 4, 5, 26, 27, 40, 41, 42, 45
              Nigel Ritchie 32
              Gerald Wood 11, 12, 22, 23

Cover photograph courtesy of UNESCO.

Acknowledgements

The author team, Northern College of Education, Aberdeen, and Ward Lock Educational Company Limited wish to acknowledge the outstanding contribution and assistance in the development of this project that has been provided by the Occidental North Sea Consortium which comprises:

Occidental Petroleum (Caledonia) Ltd;
Texaco Britain Ltd;
International Thomson Plc;
Union Texas Petroleum Ltd.

We are grateful to the following people for permission to reproduce the illustrations on the pages listed:

Aberdeen Press and Journal   14, 15
British Caledonian Helicopters   8, 9
British Petroleum Co Ltd   36
British Standards Institute   42
Drake Well Museum   38, 39
Hong Kong Tourist Authority   35 (two)
Kwik Fit Euro Ltd   18
Leyland DAF   18
Occidental Petroleum (Caledonia) Ltd   18, 19 (two)
Red Adair Co   16 (two), 17 (two)